Just Like My Dad

Tyrell Plair & Elizabeth Johnson

PLaTy Multimedia and Publishing

Copyright © 2021 by PlaTy Multimedia & Publishing

All rights reserved. No part of this book may be reproduced or used in any manner without written permission of the copyright owner except for the use of quotations in a book review. For more information, address: admin@platymm.com.

First paperback edition: April 2021

Cover Illustration by Nicholas Badila

Cover Graphic Design by James Scales

ISBN 978-1-7369686-0-4 (paperback)

ISBN 978-1-7369686-1-1 (ebook)

ISBN 978-1-7369686-2-8 (Libraries)

ISBN 978-1-7369686-9-7 (Hardback)

www.platymm.com

@platymmp

@lizzymay97

@tyrellplair_official

Contents

Acknowledgments — V

Acknowledgments — VII

1. Chapter One — 3

2. Chapter Two — 11

3. Chapter Three — 19

4. Chapter Four — 27

5. Chapter Five — 37

6. Chapter Six — 49

7. Chapter Seven — 57

8. Chapter Eight — 63

FROM THE AUTHORS	74
Elizabeth M. Johnson	76
Tyrell Plair	78
Also By Elizabeth Also By	80
Tyrell Plair	81

Acknowledgments

First and foremost, I want to thank God for everything he has done for me and for giving me the strength to author this book.

To my Heartbeats (My Parents), Wiley Charles Petteway & Arverna Petteway, I thank you for your unconditional love, support, and guidance you have shown me through the years. I would not be the woman I am today without you both. Dad, although you will not be able to hold the book physically, I know you are looking down from heaven above saying, "Well Done."

To my husband, Antonio, thank you for your love, support, and everything you do for our family. You are the wind beneath my wings.

To my son Tykel, I love you and thank you for all you do to be the best you can be. I am so blessed to be your Mom.

To Alicia and Brielle, I love you both. Thank you for allowing me to be a part of your lives.

To my spiritual mother, Bishop Gordon, thank you for your continued prayers, love, and encouragement. As you always say, "You were built for this."

To my co-author, CEO Tyrell Plair, and Alonzo Strange, Vice President of PlaTy Multimedia, thank you for believing in me and allowing me to write my first book with your company.

Lastly, to my family and friends, thank you for your continued support, love, and well wishes.

~ Elizabeth Johnson ~

Acknowledgments

I would first like to thank God for this journey and the many blessings placed before me.

A special thanks go to my parents, Valencia Johnson & Anthony Plair, and other family & friends for their continued support and encouragement.

I would also like to thank my PlaTy Multimedia team, who helped me bring my vision to light, gathering information and resources that guided us in making PlayTy Multimedia a success.

To my co-author, Elizabeth Johnson, thank you for the opportunity to work and create a teaching platform in "Just Like My Dad."

~ Tyrell Plair ~

Chapter One

"It's your turn, Daddy," Miriam shouted with joy as she shared another rare and precious moment with her dad. Her mom, Helen, watched on with sadness in her eyes, knowing that her daughter's happiness would be short-lived, and she would eventually have to pick up the pieces.

"Time for bed, Miriam." Her mom spoke barely above a whisper. Neither her daughter nor her dad moved as their eyes stayed glued to the chessboard. "Miriam, did you hear me?"

"Yes, ma'am...I was..." She stumbled over her words while still focusing on the chess game.

"Helen, at least let us finish the game... Don't be such a party pooper," Jackson stated, drawing a laugh from his small audience of one, Miriam. Her laughter stopped after seeing that her mom didn't find anything to be funny.

"Miriam, finish this game, take your bath, and go straight off to bed...is that understood young lady?" her mother stated sternly.

"Yes ma'am," she responded.

Now that Miriam was finally able to concentrate on the game without any pressure, she could finally capitalize on her "Queen's Gambit" opening that she has been studying online.

"Check," she recited, her voice calm and determined. Jackson moved his king quickly while smiling.

"Out of Check," he replied.

"Check!" This time, she stated it with emphasis. Her dad paused momentarily, then stared at the board. He placed his hand on his chin before rocking his head from side to side.

"Uhm Miriam, didn't your mother just tell you that it was time for bed?" he asked, realizing what his daughter was about to accomplish.

"She did... Get out of check, Dad." Miriam giggled with anticipation at the thought of her first real win over her dad in chess.

Most times, her dad would throw a game to teach her the game, but this time was different. *Miriam has finally done it*, he thought to himself. There was no way out of checkmate, and he knew it. It would only take two moves no matter what he did before his King was captured. Jackson smiled proudly before letting his daughter finish the game that she so rightly deserved to win. Jackson moved according to her pressure, resulting in his first loss to his daughter. Miriam sprung to her feet with excitement.

"I won! I won! I won!" she screamed while doing a series of popular dance moves. Jackson pulled out his phone to capture the precious moment. He couldn't remember the last time that he'd seen his daughter so happy.

"You did really good, Miriam; I am so proud of you. I knew that it wouldn't be long before you would be able to beat me. I want you to keep studying the game. That's what I didn't have the patience to do," he told his daughter, being honest.

"You really never had the patience to do much, Jackson," Miriam's mom stated with her arms crossed as if she was irritated. "Miriam, the game is over, now please go do as you were told," Helen ordered.

Miriam's head lowered slightly as she began the journey over to hug her dad. "Good night, Dad. I love you."

"I love you too, Lefty," he replied.

Miriam slowly proceeded to her room as her mother had instructed until Helen grabbed her arm gently. "Congratulations on finally beating your dad," she congratulated her daughter before returning her attention back to Jackson.

Helen and Jackson stared at each other in silence until they could hear their daughter's bathwater running.

"Helen, you really know how to steal a kid's joy. Miriam was excited about that win, and she deserved to be. I didn't let her win this time—she earned it," he stated before sitting back down at the chess table that he had made for his daughter.

"Well, I am glad that she won, but her winning is not the issue at hand. It is her losing in life every time that you leave for weeks at a time. You are on the road three weeks out of the month driving. It seems to me that your trucking business is all that you seem to care about. Yes, you spend precious time playing this game with your daughter, but I must play real-life with her. Let me tell you exactly what that entails, Jackson. It involves taking her to dental appointments, library trips, clothes shopping, and whatever else she needs, while you drive all over the country delivering pizza. When are you going to start putting us first and fulfill your commitment to your daughter and me?"

"First off, I do not deliver pizza, Helen, and you know that. I drive a truck that I own outright for a meat distribution company. My job provides for this family, and it also provides the means for you and Miriam to live well," Jackson replied in his own defense.

"Do you really think that it is fair that you continue to drop in on us like we're on your delivery route, checking in on us, then leaving, Jackson? Maybe I am the only one that can see that your daughter's only time of engaging with others is when you're around. Miriam remains in her room all day, embedded on her computer, watching YouTube, and playing video games."

"Helen, we spoke about this before, and I told you that I'd be getting off the road soon. What more do you want me to say? We have this same conversation over and over, and frankly, I'm tired of it," he stated, then stood up to walk off. Jackson stopped immediately as he noticed a figure just over his wife's shoulder. There, in the doorway, stood Miriam, his one and only daughter looking on as she heard every word spoken. He could see the heartache on her face.

Miriam's eyes turned red as tears began to flow. Helen quickly rushed over to console her daughter, wrapping her arms tightly around her. Her mom was the cause of Miriam's sudden sadness. She did not like to see her dad upset, and she felt sad for him. There was little response from her dad.

"I am so sorry, Miriam. I have to go," Jackson stated before walking out the door, once again proving his wife to be right.

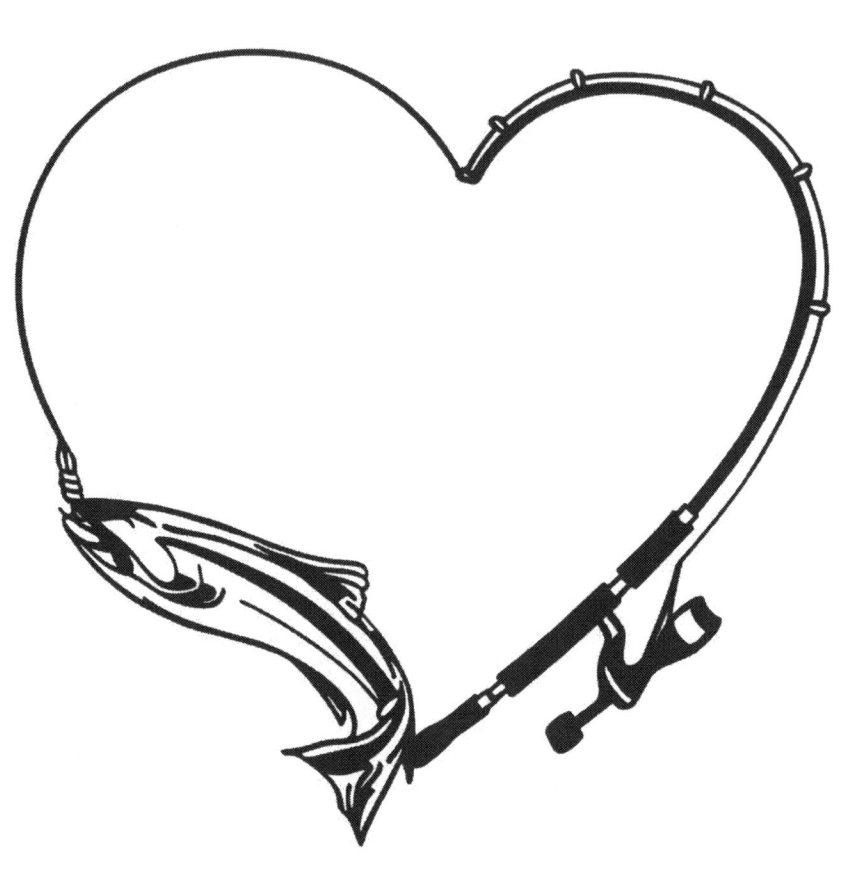

Chapter Two

"You got 'em, boy, that's a big one right there," Burt, Justin's father, commented excitedly, "Reel 'em Bucko...just like that; he'll get tuckered out here shortly."

Burt watched on with pride as his one and only son handled the fishing rod, just as he had been taught.

"I got 'em, Pops! It's a big one too... I'm not throwing this one back!"

Burt removed the fish off the hook, then handed it to his son by its large mouth, which was hanging wide open. "Stand over there son and let me get a good picture of you."

Justin slowly walked over to where the pond shone perfectly in the background. He then lifted his sunglasses and straightened his hat, all while maintaining a wide smile. He held the massive fish in the air as if it were a trophy. He extremely tall kid for a 12-year-old, standing just short of six-foot. But being tall and athletic allowed him to excel in sports at an early age, which is something he loved.

Justin lowered the fish, then held it in front of himself with two hands like a baby. "That's enough pics, Pop."

"Okay. Since you're keeping him, go ahead and place him in the cooler then. It's getting late. Time we pack it up and get you home."

"But Pop, we still have daylight... isn't that what you always tell me when I talk about wanting to leave?"

Burt chuckled at the thought of Justin using his favorite quote against him. "It's not me, Bucko. Your mom just text me and said that supper is almost ready. You know what that means, so pack it up."

"All right, Pop," Justin replied, feeling disappointed.

"Hey, it's okay. We have four days next month for the Fourth of July weekend. We talked about how tough divorce would be on us spending time, but it was for the best," Burt confessed as he followed his son over to the cooler to help him. He watched Justin pull out the largemouth bass and hurl it back into the water to his surprise.

"Now what'd you go and do that for? You still throwing temper tantrums at 12 years old?" Burt questioned as he walked over and grabbed Justin by his shirt. "What did I tell you about disrespecting me boy? You got too much of your Momma in you."

"But I wasn't disrespecting you, Pop. I didn't want the fish anymore," Justin replied, gazing into his father's eyes. He found the cold stare that he and his mother dreaded looking back at him. "I apologize, Pop if I disrespected you!" he stated, hoping to calm his dad down.

"Hey, what's going on here? Are you okay, son?" a nearby elder couple questioned as they approached the father and son duo.

Burt released his grip on his son's shirt, before responding. "Yeah, everything's just dandy in these parts. I was just having a conversation with 'MY' son," he stated with emphasis. "We raise our boys a little different than y'all do...teach them stuff other than rap and hanging out, you know?" Burt stated with unwarranted hate for the couple."

The caring couple ignored the obvious racial overtones of the man. "Son, if you need us to call someone, just let us know. We'll be close by if you need us."

"I said we were just fine and dandy...what part of that didn't y'all get? The fine or the dandy part? Justin, now go pick up that cooler and put it on the truck as I told you. Your momma's waiting on you! Now, if you don't mind, we're going to finish packing up here, so I can get him home to his momma."

At a loss for words, the elder couple nodded in agreement. They glanced back often as they made distance between themselves and the father and son duo. The elders said a silent prayer that focused on the young man having a better future than what his dad was providing. Their hopes were that he would not grow up to be, just like his dad.

Justin waited until he thought the couple was a good distance away before speaking. He could still see them looking back at them. "Dad, why were you so rude to those old people?" Justin questioned upon entering the passenger seat of his dad's truck.

Burt looked at his son, who was the perfect likeness to him in every way, except in the way that he thought. "Are you saying that telling those people to mind their business was being rude? Let me tell you what's rude. Rude is when people let their kids grow up wearing baggy clothes, talk with slang, and end up in prison. No one can tell me how to raise my son. I hate that your mom moved you out here where there's so many of them. This kind of environment is a recipe for a crime, just so you know. I do not want you becoming all hip-hop either, since I'm not around as much. Remember what I taught you, Son. You do still want to be like your dad, right?" Burt questioned as he rubbed his son's head to lighten the mood.

Justin sat briefly in thought, before responding. Although he did not see things the way his dad did, he did understand where he was coming from. Justin was well aware of the consequences that would ensue if his dad didn't get the answer he sought, so he was very careful with his response.

"You don't have to worry about that Pops. The closest thing to rap music that I'll listen to is Billy Ray Cyrus." Justin was even more careful with his follow-up statement. "I don't think all black people are bad though, we've played baseball against them a few times, even in the last championship game."

Burt looked over at him with a wry smile on his face. "See Son, you've just proved my point. Weren't you the main person complaining after last year's loss, about how they cheated you guys? I specifically remember you stating that all 'they' do is cheat. The proof is in the pudding, Son. You used to be just like me in so many ways; has something changed since then?"

Justin peered at his dad, who indeed was looking for an answer. "I am just like you, Dad. I mean, I try to be," he stated, being honest.

"Good...I see great things ahead for you, Son," Burt proudly stated as he drove his son home, satisfied with the role he plays in Justin's life.

Chapter Three

"Hey, how's it going, Coach Carl? How many have you signed up for baseball so far?"

"Right now, we need about four more kids, which will be enough to kick off the season. I'm sure a few will come out as the restrictions for the pandemic lessen, Mike."

Coach Mike took a deep breath before taking a seat next to his old friend, who was now in charge of monitoring the registration booth. "I'll tell you this Coach, this isn't like registration in the days when we came up playing summer sports. We used to love being outside. As a matter of fact, I remember my mom having to yell for us to come in from playing football in the dark. All these kids nowadays want to do is, play video games and make funny videos."

"Well, it's nothing wrong with that, Mike. I play video games too; I just don't make funny videos. The reality is that parents think that they do not have the time to invest in supporting their children, in their athletic endeavors. So, in turn, they don't sign them up. I mean, why sign them up, only to disappoint them with a reason you couldn't make their game?" Coach Carl reasoned.

"I understand what you are saying Coach, and no it is not the same," Coach Mike replied.

"That is why this might be my last year coaching. Think about it coach. With the pandemic, and a few select parents willing to let their children get back involved in sports; this might be the league's last season. I think that might be time for me to bow out gracefully. We have several new young coaches around here, that I'm sure would be eager to Coach the Braves."

Mike took off his ball cap, which exposed his bald head, and stared at his friend in disbelief. "You mean to tell me that you're really about to quit? Quit for what, Coach? Just give me a good reason... and before you do, let me remind you that the outlet we were given when we were kids is the same one that we're to provide here." Coach Carl's expression softened at the all too true statement.

"Even if that is the case, Coach, you have no idea what I have going on outside of coaching. I for one realize that life doesn't begin and end here at Lincoln Park field coaching baseball. You truly have no idea," Coach Carl responded, speaking his truth.

"What makes you think I don't? I was right by your side when you lost your family. I was also here when you started back coaching, finding yourself again; just as your wife and daughter would have wanted you to do. Let me ask you something, Coach. Do you have any idea how rare it is for someone our age to still have a community to go to? Let alone to be able to coach sports?"

"I do know how rare that is. Through gentrification, communities like ours have been torn down for lucrative businesses or fancy properties that most residents cannot afford. We barely had enough kids to play summer sports before the pandemic, and now we have cut it down to four teams, in each sport. We are basically becoming babysitters as we try to give the kids something to do. We've lost four coaches in the process! I know if I were a kid, I'd be tired of playing the same kids every week, especially since we have travel restrictions in place," Coach Carl stated as he made every excuse to leave coaching.

Coach Mike wasn't convinced. He stood up and took a long stretch before looking down at his friend and speaking. "I will tell you this, and you know my story Coach. I lost my mom when I was five, and my dad when I was eleven. My grandparents took me in shortly after my dad's passing. As you know, my grandfather brought me to this same field and registered me for summer sports. From that day forward, I developed an uncanny love for the game that has allowed me to go to college on a full scholarship. See, my goal was never to play professionally; it was to obtain an education, that my parents weren't there to help me get. Anything after my college education was like icing on the cake. I've always tried to live up to my dad's expectations as he was a good man all around. I'd be the first to tell you that, and it's no secret; I wanted to be just like my dad."

Coach Carl took a deep breath as he knew his friend's story all too well. "Coach, do you know that I've started seeing a counselor?"

"I'm not surprised. I used to see one, right up until the eleventh grade. After that I was aware of the things I needed to grow as an individual," he replied.

"I keep thinking about what might have been, and it is depressing. I used to get so excited about the coaching season, but this season it felt more like a burden. It shouldn't feel like that, Coach." The frustration coming from Coach Carl was evident.

Coach Mike placed his hand on his friend's shoulder to console him. "Coach, I'm not sure what's going on with you right now, but I for one don't want to see you go back to that place of isolation. I would never tell a man to do something, that I wouldn't do, but just promise me that you will let this season help you decide your future in coaching. You never know, something might just change your mind to where you fall back in love with coaching."

"I'll give you my word that I will let this season determine my coaching decision, but I doubt that my decision will change."

"Coach Carl, you of all people know that negative thinking brings about negative results. You'll be telling your team that same quote in a matter of days." They both fell out laughing at the truthful statement. "You're not going to be able to give this up, Coach...this is good times at its finest," Coach Mike told him wholeheartedly.

"Good times don't last long...always remember that."

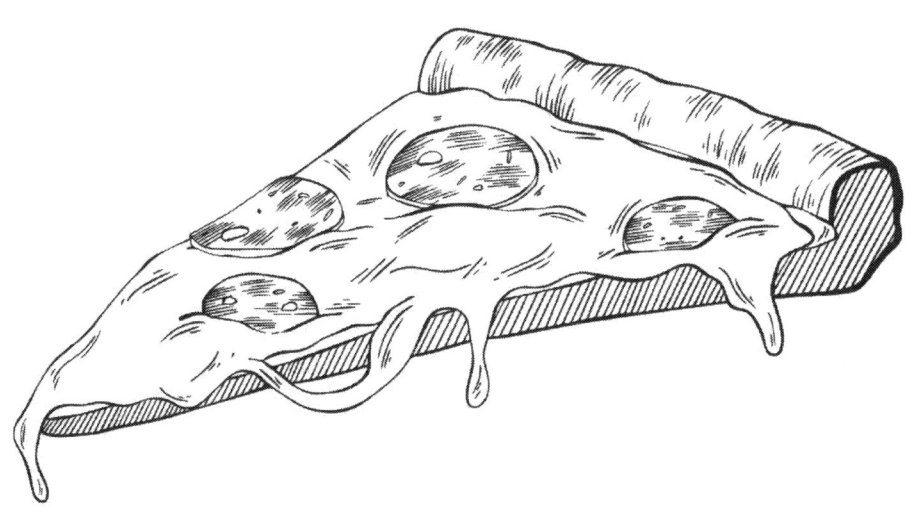

Chapter Four

"Desmond, can you take the pizza out of the oven?" his mom called out to him from the laundry room as she removed the clothes out of the dryer.

"Mom, can't it wait, I'm online playing the game?" he yelled back to her.

Carla had had enough of repeating herself each time that she asked her son to do something. She recognized that Desmond was at an age where his influences became greater by the day. At 12 years old, most kids are often encouraged by their environments, and peers thereof. The line has been drawn for most to either choose to be bad or choose to be good; there was no in-between.

"Look, Desmond, I am in here folding clothes that you claim you can't do yourself. I am so tired of repeating myself when I ask you to do something. Now, go take that pizza out of the oven before you burn my house down!" Carla ordered.

Lately, Carla had become highly frustrated with the behavior of her one and only son. She noticed that Desmond had become stuck in a non-productive routine of coming home from school and running straight to his room. His room was never clean, and his life revolved around playing video games. He had no friends that she knew of, other than his online friends, due to his introverted nature.

"Okay, Mom, doing it now," he replied.

Carla folded the last of the clothes, then placed them in the clothes hamper. The smell of burnt pizza began to waft through her nostrils. She immediately called out to her son as she ran out of the laundry room with the hopes that her kitchen was not on fire.

"Desmond!" she called out his name once again in a panic. Carla made it to the kitchen in time to notice, that a large amount of smoke was seeping out of the oven door. She turned the oven off and then opened its door. A massive cloud of dark smoke began pouring out. The dark cloud floated smoothly over Desmond's head as he entered the room, breathing hard.

"Mom, what happened?" Desmond questioned as he held his video game controller in his hand tightly. He followed his mother's gaze down to his left hand that held the video game controller.

"Hand it here now, and don't make me ask you again, Desmond!" she beckoned with her hand held out.

"But Mom, I was just about to..." He never got a chance to finish his statement as his mother surprised him by snatching the controller out of his hand. Carla followed it up by slamming it on the kitchen table. Parts to which Desmond knew to be necessary to his controller flew in all different directions.

"Mom, you just..." He was cut off again from speaking. A pattern he knew all too well now.

"Do you think I care about a game controller? It could have been burned up in here, with the both of us, due to your negligence. Do you have any idea what could've happened had I not been here, Desmond? You are irresponsible, and for you to think that you can sit around here and do what you want to do like the world owes you something is self-pity. I have been very patient with you ever since your dad's passing," she stated. Desmond's face instantly lowered.

"Mom, do we have to talk about this now? I am really sorry for leaving the pizza in the oven. It won't happen again."

"You can bet it won't happen again as far as I am concerned. Have a seat—and yes, we're going to talk about this now," she told him before joining him at the kitchen table. The smoke from the burned pizza was now a thin film that was dispersing. "Desmond, I have watched you fall into a routine that has made you a shell of the young man you were becoming. Before your dad's passing, you were always engaged, always looking forward to going outside. Now, all you do is come home and play video games. You have been overeating with no exercise, which has caused you to gain weight. The main concern that I have is your constant disobedience and lack of effort for things that benefit you. Had you just gotten up to check the pizza that you asked me to put on, we wouldn't be having this conversation—but I'm glad it happened."

"You're glad that I burned the pizza?" Desmond questioned, confused.

"No silly... I'm glad that, based on you not listening, we were forced to have this conversation. Everything happens for a reason, always remember that."

Desmond rubbed his hands over his stomach while looking down. He noticed that his belly was slightly poking out. He held it in tight before speaking. "Mom, my stomach is not that big. Maybe I'm just bloated as I hear you say sometimes when you look in the mirror."

A huge smile formed on his face. Carla could barely contain her laughter, even in such a serious teaching moment. "You're not bloated, and please don't ever repeat that to anyone, Son. The point is, you're at an age where you need to be out engaging with other kids your age; kids that are active mentally and physically. Your dad would be disappointed that you're not playing some sport."

"Okay. Well, how about I try out for something next year? This way, I can have it all planned out. Right now, it seems kinda rushed, Mom. I'll grab another pizza out of the deep freezer, and this time I'll sit in here until it is done," Desmond stated, believing that his plan of action would end the conversation.

"Not so fast mister... Hand me my purse that's on the kitchen counter." Desmond hurriedly retrieved the purse, maintaining a smile that would captivate the meanest crowd.

"Here you go Mom, anything else?"

"Yes, have a seat. I didn't tell you that I was done in the first place." Carla opened her purse, retrieved a folded piece of paper, and then slid it gently across the table to her son.

"What is it?" he questioned, staring at it as if it were not to be touched.

"Open it up and see," she coaxed.

Desmond picked up the piece of paper, opened it, and began reading silently. When he finished reading, he folded the paper back up and slid it back to his mom; the same way she had given it to him.

"Well?" she questioned curiously.

"Well, what?"

"Well, those are the three summer sports programs that you can sign up for. Let's be clear, the only reason I'm giving you a choice in the matter is that I want you to want to do this. I should not have to force you to be more active, or to start acting as a young man should. Registration is today, and we're going down to the park, to get you registered for either summer basketball, football, or baseball," she declared. "You can think about it while you're getting dressed."

"Mom, are you serious? Like, this is the first week of summer!"

"Desmond, this is not up for debate. Seeing that you won't have any video games to play, I would like to think that you would be excited about being able to get out of the house."

"What do you mean, I won't have any video games to play?" he questioned, confused.

"It means exactly what I said, Desmond. From this day forward, your video game playing days are over; at least until I see some changed behavior. I have one broken controller here... Would you like to make it a broken console as well?"

"Okay, Mom, I'm going to get it," he stated, while still sitting in place, wearing a scowl.

"This right here is the problem. You still want to do things when *you* want to do them. Even after I just asked you to bring me the rest of the video game, you choose to sit there."

Desmond sprung to his feet. "I'm going, Mom," he stated, sounding frustrated. He returned with the game console within minutes and placed it on the table next to the broken controller. "Here, I brought it to you."

"Thank you, Son. Miriam's mother also signed her up to play summer sports, so you might get a chance to see your cousin more often."

"Miriam? Playing sports? Please tell me that you're kidding, Mom," he stated, unbelievingly.

"I'm not. Why would I make this up? Miriam was just as surprised when I told her that you would be playing sports this summer as well. You and your cousin have some of the same issues, and my sister and I think it is best to try something different. I think playing sports can and will do you both some good," his mom replied, knowing how he would take his cousin jabbing at him.

"Well, I have never witnessed her play anything, other than chess at school they call her, Boring Lauren. What made Miriam want to play sports? Is she being forced too?"

"I don't know," she replied when it was a known fact that she very well why his cousin was being placed into sports—for the same reason that he was. They were both becoming shells of themselves, only consumed with doing the same thing every day. There was no mental or physical growth insight to be had by taking this path.

"Well, I don't care what sport she ends up playing, she'll end up being my cheerleader anyway," Desmond stated with all the confidence in the world. He was now, excited about signing up, even if the excitement was only to show his cousin Miriam up. "I'll be ready in twenty minutes, Mom, and thank you," he stated as he walked over and wrapped his arms around his mother's body.

"I knew you could be a sweetheart," she stated, happy that her son had agreed to sign up willingly.

Carla continued to smile as she watched her son walk out of the kitchen. She truly hoped that placing her son in the hands of some positive men would do him wonders. For Desmond, acquiring the discipline and the enthusiasm that a young child should possess was all that she wanted in return.

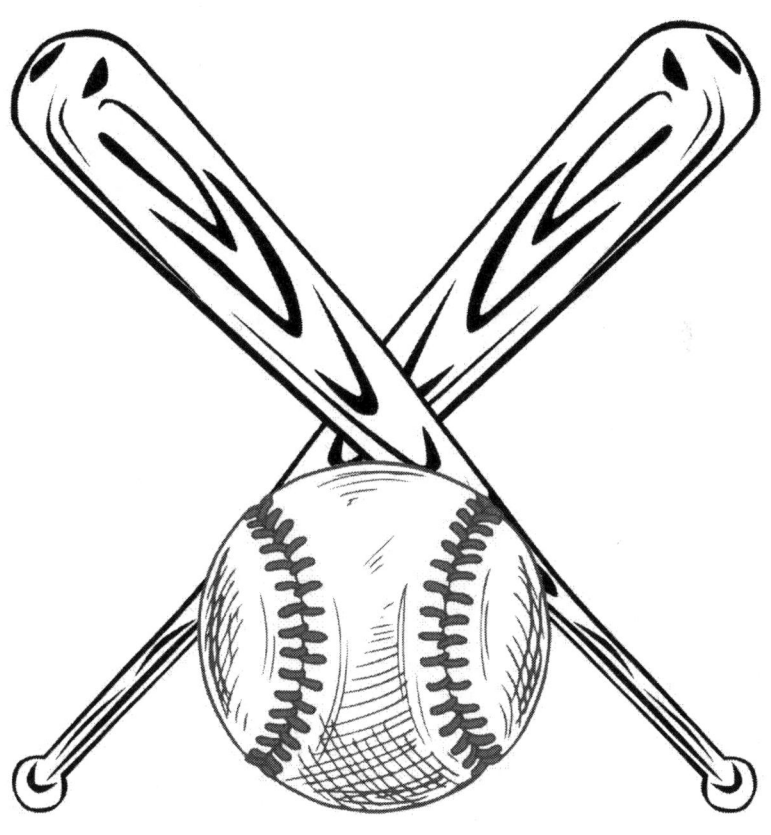

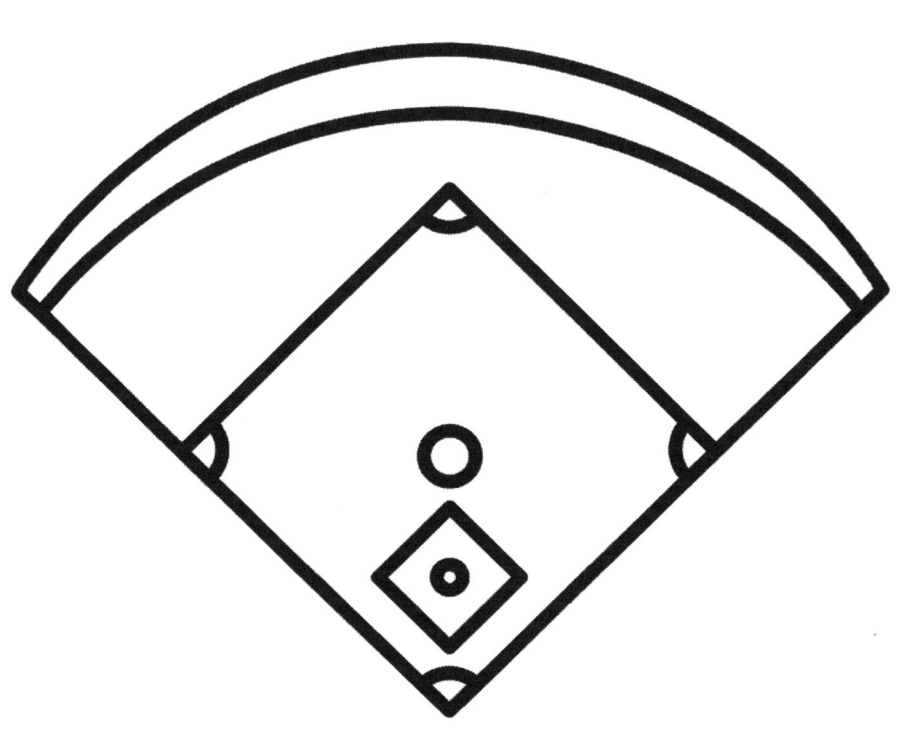

Chapter Five

"All right, let's get lined up. Everyone on the line facing the outfield. When I point at you, I want you to state your name and what position you would like to play. If you hear someone say the position that you want to play, don't worry about it. Every position on this team is earned. For those that don't know, my name is Coach Carl, and this is my assistant, Coach Mike. Coach Mike and I, played baseball, at this very same park when we were kids." A few laughs escaped from some of the kids.

"What seems to be so funny?" Coach Mike questioned as he scanned the line full of preteens for an answer.

"So y'all must not have a life. You played here, and now you want to coach here too? I mean, does anyone else see a problem with these two?" the attention-seeking player stated.

Coach Carl looked over at the parking lot where most parents stood, socially distanced, while watching their children practice. "We're going to get one thing straight before we go any further. At no time is it okay for players to insult one another, or a coach, with the hopes of trying to get a laugh. Getting a laugh at someone else's expense can be taken as being mean, and disrespectful. We are a team that can have fun, but we will not do it at the expense of another team or teammate. Is everyone on board with me?"

They replied just as they did before in unison, except this time they added 'Coach Carl'.

"Coach Mike, could you proceed with the introductions, please?"

Coach Carl requested, while he folded his arms and studied each kid that stood in front of him. This year was the first time that he had, such a diverse group of kids. Coach Carl noticed that there was even a young lady that stood before him, ready to play and learn hopefully. The coach was now curious about each kid's level of experience, which was one of the most exciting parts of coaching.

"The name of our team is called the Lincoln Park Braves. Let me tell you what my definition of the word 'brave' is. Being brave is having the heart and courage to face any opponent that comes your way without fear. Wouldn't you agree?"

Everyone agreed by saying "yes" in unison.

"Good stuff. Now, who do we have here?" he questioned as he pointed at a kid that was standing there with a blank stare. "Are you here with us, young man?"

"Yeah...I mean, yes Coach, I'm here." The kid spoke with uncertainty as he adjusted his glasses on his nose before asking. "What was the question?" He glanced over to the parking lot once more—as if he was looking for someone—then returned his attention to his coach.

"I asked if you would state your name and the position that you would like to play." Coach Mike spoke to him with patience.

It was obvious the kid was nervous. "Hey, Coach Mike, we can come back to him, while he thinks about the position that he wants to play." Coach Carl stated, showing empathy as he was once that same nervous kid. His nervousness disappeared as he turned out to be a star in baseball. Coach Carl wasn't too sure if this kid would turn out the same.

"What is your name, young man?" Coach Mike continued.

"I'm Desmond, and I can play any position," he stated as he looked down the line at his cousin, Miriam. Both coaches noticed their subtle eye contact.

"Since Desmond, looked at you when he spoke, how about you introduce yourself, young lady." Coach Mike suggested.

"Hi, my name is Miriam. That is my no-clue-how-to-play-sports cousin that just introduced himself. I can play any position in the outfield, but I prefer left field," she replied, surprising everyone with her knowledge of the game.

"Yeah, well, we don't need no girl in the outfield that will require two cut-off men to get it to second base," Justin stated snidely, drawing laughter. Justin took the laughter as motivation to continue his insults. "Like, if I had known we were going to have a team of girls, I would've stayed with my last team." He laughed even harder at his own statements, which prompted everyone else to stop.

"Hey, that's my cousin that you're talking about!" Desmond stated as he started making his way toward the extremely tall kid but was stopped by Coach Mike.

"Whoa... now, this is what we're *not* about to do. We are just stating names and positions now. Your opinion of what someone will or will not do is not up to either of you. You'll never know what a person is capable of; especially if you go by their outer appearance. Anyone who has watched Allen Iverson play should know that." Most of the kids looked at him with confusion in their eyes.

Coach Carl let out a chuckle. "Coach Mike, maybe you should've mentioned Steph Curry instead." The kids' faces lit up with acknowledgment. "As Coach Mike was saying, underestimating anyone will be doing yourself a disservice. When you take your opponent for granted, that means that you train as if the fight or battle has already been won. But, if you think that there is a chance that you might lose, you will train, and do what it takes to give yourself a chance. You have to believe with every opponent that thinks the same way, so never can I take anything or anyone for granted. Okay, let us continue. It looks like we have about two more players."

One more introduction was made before it was now back on the young man, who continued to look off into the parking lot every so often. "Tell us your name, then tell me who you keep looking for out in that parking lot," Coach Mike said.

He leaned forward and looked down the line at his new teammates. He gave a slight smile, which could have been considered a smirk under different circumstances. The young man, then stepped out in front of his teammates confidently. He gave them all a glance-over before speaking.

"My name is Tyler, and I pitch as well," he stated without targeting anyone with his statement. "I also play any position in the infield. And lastly, the reason I keep looking into the parking lot is that I told my mom that I really didn't want to play any sports this summer," he stated with respect.

Coach Carl took the young man's statement to heart, but he also knew that there was more to the story. "Is there a reason that you don't want to play baseball; I'm assuming that it is a sport that you enjoy playing?"

"I won't be able to play with my old teammates, and this team doesn't look like it will be winning many games…especially if he's going to be our pitcher," Tyler stated as he looked Justin in his eyes.

"We beat that trash team of yours, didn't we?" Justin boasted.

"Yeah, but not when it counted. You do remember Justin, who held up the MVP trophy and Championship trophy, right?" Tyler countered. Justin became angered.

"I take it that you two have played at the same recreational park before?" Coach Mike questioned, already knowing the answer.

"Yeah, we played his team for the summer league championship when I lived in Marietta. We moved out here after my mom and—" He paused briefly. "That doesn't matter… What matters is that all those kids did was cheat and argue," Justin replied with disdain.

Coach Carl had finally had enough of acting as if he didn't notice something strange, about how Justin kept referring to certain people when he spoke. The Coach did not want to assume anything, so the right thing to do, was to ask, which he did. "Justin, can you tell me what you meant when you stated that those kids cheat all the time?"

Justin became quiet, something that had already seemed odd to everyone, given his talkative nature. It was a tricky question to process for a kid, who had never thought about answering a question, like the one that he was being asked. Justin found it strange and uncomfortable.

"Them..." he stated while pointing at Tyler. "People like him."

"Justin, I need to know that you're not using racial undertones when you say, 'People like him' or 'Them'. Those words can be taken out of context from others and could possibly make a person feel threatened or intimidated by you. Everyone here has just introduced him or herself, and we will treat everyone here equally, regardless of race or gender. The only thing that anyone should care about is, the fact that you are now a part of a team. We will be a team that picks each other up when they are down, and that shows each other mutual respect. Are we all on the same page here, guys?" Coach Carl questioned as he found an opportunity to apply a teaching moment with his new players.

Justin and Tyler stared at each other briefly while everyone else replied.

"Tyler and Justin, what Coach just asked you warrants a response—give him one. Before you do, let's be clear, this is a voluntary summer program that you kids were signed up for. Neither Coach Carl nor I forced you to sign up. The way that you conduct yourself at home with your parents is their issue, but the way you conduct yourself while you're a Brave is our issue. And the conduct expected here will be the same across the board. So, are you guys on board or not?"

"I'm on board, Coach," Tyler stated, half-heartedly.

"I just want to play ball; I don't really care about the rest," Justin replied.

The coaches took Justin's statement for what it was worth. They both were tenured coaches, which realized team sports had a way of bringing people together emotionally, physically, and mentally.

"Today we will do a little bit of fielding and throwing. Also as Coach Carl stated, we are a team, so we do everything together. Before every practice, we will do a series of stretches to loosen up the joints and muscles, which prevents injuries. We will follow that up with a jog around the outfield, or a sprint around the base pads."

"Come on, Coach. We'll be too tired to do anything after that!" Desmond replied, thinking about the running part particularly.

"After that, we'll warm up our arms by throwing to a teammate," Coach Carl continued, not acknowledging the interruption. "What is your name again, young man?" he asked as he approached his interrupter.

"Desmond...Desmond Clark Jr., or D.J," he stated proudly.

"Desmond, Desmond J, or J.D." Coach Carl, intentionally messed up his name.

"No, it's Desmond or..."

"I didn't hear you correctly when you were stating it. A fly was interrupting me." All the kids looked at him as if he had lost his mind. "Why is it that when I state that a fly distracted me, I get all the curious looks. What if Tyler or Miriam had told me that they couldn't hear what I was saying because Desmond Junior was interrupting?" All their young faces brightened as if a light bulb had just come on. "When you are in any conversation and someone is speaking, you should listen to hear vs. listening to respond. Okay, enough life lessons for today. Let's take the field and stretch. Everyone head out to centerfield." The team immediately took off running toward centerfield as if they were trying to win a race.

"Good speech, Coach. They usually don't get that kind of speech until mid-season," Coach Mike joked.

"This is true Coach, but this is a different group of kids. I can tell this group will be unlike any other team we've coached."

"Are you talking talent-wise or issues like we had today?" Coach Mike questioned.

"Both...I hope you're up for it."

"You're the one with all the retiring talk. One thing's for sure Coach; you can count on me to teach these kids all that I know about baseball. And if that means providing life lessons as you just did a few minutes ago, then so be it, friend."

"I appreciate you, Mike. I still don't know how we are still joined at the hip after all these years," Coach Carl commented, grateful for their long-standing friendship which has stood the test of time.

"Like we always say, Coach... Sports have a way of bringing the strangest of people together."

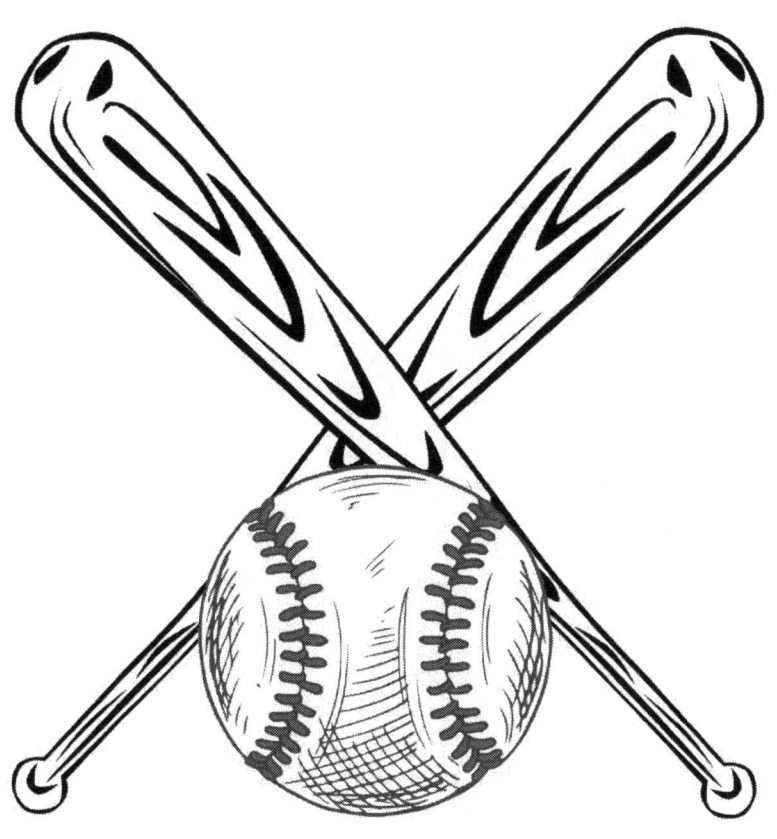

Chapter Six

"Well, good morning to you too, mister. What seems to be your problem?" Justin's mother stated, bewildered as to why her son would come to the breakfast table with the same attitude, that he had displayed last night.

"I don't have a problem," he flatly replied.

"Well yes, you do have a problem, and you are about to add to it if you keep being disrespectful. I tolerated your behavior last night after you got home from practice, but it will not carry over today. For you to think you can continue to walk around here like you are mad at the world is not right. People should always talk about what is bothering them, and not show it by pouting and slamming things down. No matter how mad a person gets, they should always use self-control and know how to conduct themselves. You are doing the opposite of that, Justin."

"I'm just tired of people talking smack."

She sat down the pot of coffee and turned to her son. She was curious as to what her son meant, by people talking smack. She hoped that he wasn't getting bullied by anyone. "Hey, is something going on that I need to know about...is someone bothering you?"

He gave her a questioning look. "No, Mom, no one is bothering me, and if they were I'd handle them," he stated in the likeness of his dad.

"You sound just like your dad. Handling them," she used her fingers to sign air quotes as she spoke, "is something that should not be in your vocabulary at this point in your life. I think I need to have another talk with your dad."

"Another talk about what?" He sounded surprised.

"A talk about your temperament, your behavior, and the words that come out of your mouth. They are so offensive and hurtful at times. Whether you know it or not, these are the same characteristics that forced your father and me to become separated, and ultimately, divorced. Your father has a way of thinking that is not acceptable today nor should it ever be. And it has a lot to do with how he was raised. Now that does not necessarily make your father a bad person, but it does give people a reason not to want to be around him."

"What do you mean? Dad has tons of friends..."

"You're right, Justin. All of your dad's friends act alike, think alike, and talk alike. Son, it's time that I talk to you about why your dad and I are no longer married. As you know, I came from a bi-racial family, although I do not look like I do. I grew up in a predominately, Caucasian neighborhood in the suburbs, and that is where I met your father. Your dad and I dated for several months before he finally came to my home. Burt found out that I had an African American father and refused to come into the house. I found out that I was pregnant with you a week later. I did my best to make it work against my family's advice. I ultimately refused, to continue to grow up, with the same way of thinking that is rooted in the belief that you are better than someone else due to your skin color, status in life, or education level."

"Mom, I don't think I'm better than anybody. I just say all that stuff, because it gets people rattled."

"What is the point of getting people rattled?"

"I watched Dad, and his friends do. They laugh about it."

"But they're laughing at someone else's expense. Tell me, what happened yesterday at practice that had you in a not-so-good mood afterward?"

His face dropped slightly before sharing, "Coach Carl, accused me of using racial undertones after he overheard Tyler and me talking... Well, arguing."

"Did he accuse Tyler of using racial undertones as well?"

"No," he replied simply, which led her to know the reason.

"Justin, something is not adding up. Let me call Coach Carl and see what this is all about."

Justin sprung to his feet. "No, Mom! I mean, don't call him. I'll tell you what I said," he stated convincingly. "I referred to Tyler, and his old team as 'Them People'. Coach then asked me what I meant by that? I didn't really mean anything by it; I hear Dad say it all the time."

A sad realization came over her, and she instantly felt a knot forming in the pit of her stomach. Never in her wildest dreams would she think that Burt would teach their son the same outdated thought process of people being different, and one race being better. Everyone is created equal and should be treated as such.

"Justin, I am deeply saddened to hear that your dad has exposed you to the way he and his associates think. The world is made of unique individuals. Regardless of what they look like, a person should only be judged by his character. You can meet someone that looks just like you, who will do you just as wrong as someone that doesn't."

Justin listened intently to the words that his mother was speaking. In his mind, he knew that what he had been saying was wrong, and it was unfair to the kids or people that he was around at the time. *Wrong is wrong*, no matter where it takes place. He realized at that point his mom was right.

"I won't use those kinds of words again, Mom. I promise," Justin told his Mom with all honesty.

"Good. I think I'm still going to call Coach Carl and speak with him. I do not want him to think that you are being taught this type of behavior at home."

"But Mom! We just talked about this."

She ignored his plea as she dialed Coach Carl's number. The phone rang twice before he picked up. "Hey, good evening, Coach Carl. This is Justin's mom, Gayle. We met the other day at practice."

"Hey Gayle, how is everything going... Is everything all right?" he questioned, curious about the purpose of the phone call.

"Well, everything is fine. I want to talk to you about Justin and his actions the other day at practice. I sincerely want to apologize for his behavior. I would say that he wasn't raised like that, but that wouldn't be totally true. Justin has been taught many negative things by his father, which contrasts with how I want him raised. His father and I are no longer together, but he has joint custody, which still allows him to project negative thoughts and words into his impressionable son."

"Ma'am, I can assure you that I have been around kids that don't hold back when it comes to their thoughts. I don't think Justin has a bad bone in his body, per se. I do think that he has been exposed to a prehistoric way of thinking, that he has not learned how to process yet. Our team is as diverse as it has ever been this year. I greatly appreciate the phone call. Do not worry about the other kids or any of the coaches viewing Justin as anything other than what he is: a baseball player."

"That is good to hear, Coach. Justin is here next to me, listening with a huge smile on his face. Would you like to speak with your coach, Justin?" He grabbed the phone, readily accepting her offer.

"Hey, what's up Coach?" Justin, walked away from his mother, to where he thought he was out of her earshot. "I'm sorry my mom had to call you. I hope that you know that I'm not like that coach. As Mom stated, I learned a lot from my dad, and I really wanted to be like my dad. Now that I know that the things my dad says and does are not always right, I had a change of heart. I want to be like him still in some ways, just not in that way," Justin professed.

"Justin, you're a smart kid, and when we choose someone to be like, we must first ask ourselves if that person is worth emulating. We spoke briefly about this the other day at practice. Tell your mom that I appreciate the phone call, and I'll see you at practice tomorrow."

"You got it, Coach. ...and Coach? Thank you for everything."

"For what?"

"For showing me that I can be like my dad, but I can choose in which ways once I recognize them."

Chapter Seven

"Let's go, Tyler, you're going to be late for practice!"

"I'm coming, Mom. I'm just grabbing my cleats. I was talking to Dad," he called out to his mother from his bedroom. He walked down the steps to see his mother sitting on the couch.

"Mom, come on, I thought we were going to be late?" he asked as he opened the front door.

"Close the door for a minute Tyler and come have a seat." He walked over slowly to where his mom sat and took a seat next to her.

"What's up Mom, did I do something wrong?" he questioned as his mind tried to recall if he had indeed done something wrong recently.

"Not yet, you haven't. Tyler, I watched you at the last practice, and I don't want what happened last time to happen here. You can't keep getting into conflicts every time that you go, and then blame others for it."

"But Mom, I didn't..." she cut him off.

"Tyler, I would prefer you not interrupt me again while I'm speaking, or anyone else for that matter. You will never be able to hear what anyone is trying to say if you are thinking about how you need to respond. Respect is always given, but to earn respect requires honorable behavior, and your behavior of late doesn't warrant anyone's respect."

"Mom, can whatever it is that I did, or that you think I did, wait until after practice?" He stood up as if that would end the conversation.

"I just spoke to you about respect. You don't have to be in a rush. One of the reasons that I'm speaking to you now is because I spoke with Coach Carl."

Tyler placed his baseball equipment back on the floor and took a seat as he knew that would be his mother's next instruction. "About what?" he asked as if he were clueless.

"He told me about you and another player on your team exchanging words. Tyler, this is unlike you to keep getting into these little spats. I'm not sure from where this newly learned behavior comes, from because you sure didn't get it from your dad or me."

Tyler's facial expression changed, and his mother immediately noticed as his words confirmed his thoughts. "You're right, Mom, I'm nothing like my dad because I don't have one...and you and I both know why."

Her heart was crushed at her son's last statement. She knew that Tyler held a long-standing resentment toward his father that was unwarranted. Whereas most dads readily give up the opportunity to help be a part of their children's lives as they fall prey to a harmful lifestyle, that wasn't the case with Tyler's dad. Terrence was a devoted dad, whose loyalty to his family's lifestyle led him to take a life sentence for a crime he did not commit.

"Tyler, you truly have no idea how much you are like your dad. Your father has a character that most people would envy, and he truly lived by his values, which is why he is in prison, and not with us today. He protected your Uncle Darrell, and that is why you aren't allowed around him."

A newfound resentment formed for his uncle as he began to understand the phone conversation that he had with him. "Uncle Darrell is the one who told me the story of how Dad shouldn't be in prison, and that he should be out here enjoying life, with me. I asked him what he meant by that, and he never said anything. So, Dad is in prison because of Uncle Darrell?" he asked, putting the story together.

"Yes," she stated regretfully.

Tyler studied the sadness on his mother's face. No child wants to see their mother hurt, so he did what any child would do, wrapped his arms around her, and held on tight.

"Dad will be home one day Mom, I know it," he stated with confidence.

"That would be so nice, Son. That would be so nice."

Tyler held on to his mother tightly as he thought about his dad never enjoying life as a free man again due to his Uncle Darrell's actions. A wave of emotion overtook him, and he found himself sobbing just as hard as his mother.

"Mom, I know Dad wants to come home...and one day he will. He told me that."

His mother lifted her head from her son's shoulder. She held his head in her hands as she looked into his eyes. This was news to her, being that his dad had long ago accepted doing a life sentence, to protect his brother. "Did your dad tell you that?"

"Yes. He told me that a lawyer was working on his case and that one day he'll be home."

This was great news, which turned her sad tears into tears of hope and joy. "I love you Son, and until your dad comes home, I need you to be just like him: responsible and loving."

"I will, Mom. I promise." Tyler meant every word.

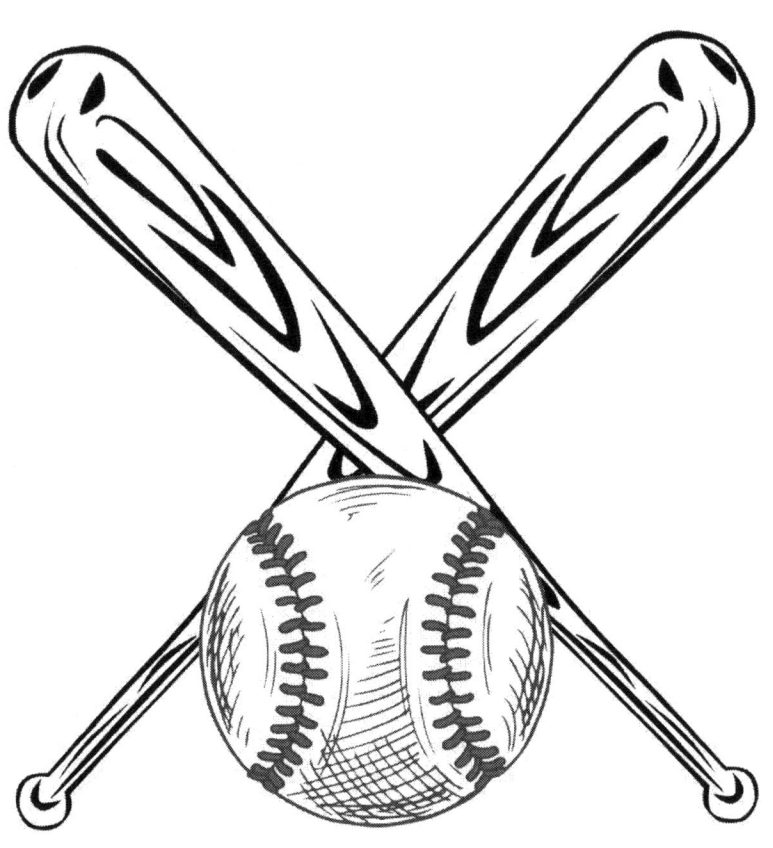

Chapter Eight

"All right, line it up. You already know what it is." Coach Carl gathered his players together as they had finally made it to their first game of the season. "Today is the day that we see if all of our hard work at practice pays off. This is where teammates solidify themselves as being able to be depended upon. Baseball is a team sport that will require the use of your cognitive skills, athletic skills, and communication skills all at the same time... and that might be just on one play," Coach Carl stated emphatically.

Coach Mike chimed in, adding, "As Coach Carl stated, to have success as a team, we have to operate like a well-oiled machine. We have practiced very hard, and we have settled our differences all for this very day." Coach Mike spoke proudly as he scanned over his players. Then, he noticed someone missing. "Hey, where's Miriam?"

No one had paid any attention to Miriam's absence as she was often sitting off quietly mentally preparing herself.

"Desmond, where's your cousin at, bro? It's almost game time," Tyler asked, which triggered the rest of the team to begin uttering their concerns.

"Hey guys, hold up a second. I know everyone is getting frustrated with where Miriam is but we have enough players to start the game, and I am confident in the players I have here. We have another five minutes before game time. As of now, Desmond, you will be starting in centerfield instead of left field. Ricky, you will play left field and bat ninth." Coach Carl laid out his plan of execution.

"We're starting the season all wrong, Coach. All practice season, you talked to us about being committed to this team and to each other to win. We all know that Miriam is not just someone that can easily be replaced, and that's no knock on you either, Desmond." Justin nodded in his teammate's direction in a show of respect, before confessing. "But her arm strength, bat, and speed are what we built our lineup and game plan off. Coach, I know that when I'm pitching, I don't worry about a ball being hit to her, and now it's just..." Justin stated, letting his feelings be heard.

Coach Carl walked over and placed his hand on Justin's shoulder. "Hey, I need everyone to bring it in and take a knee."

He watched on as each player sat their baseball glove on the ground, then placed their knee on top of it while maintaining an upright posture. Everything that he had taught them so far, he noticed was being retained.

"I remember the first day that you kids showed up here for your first day of practice. There was no unity, no humility among each other, and a huge lack of discipline and respect. I can honestly say that each one of those things has been corrected or changed in a way that shows more of your character. I have confidence in each of you to do your job and pick up the slack when needed. Yes, Miriam is one of our best players and is great at the top of the lineup, but she is not here. In life, there will be all kinds of things that disappoint you, family and friends included. It's not about if or when they will disappoint you, it is all about how you," he pointed at his players for emphasis, "respond to it. We talk about overcoming adversity all the time, and today will be no exception."

"Coach, they're asking for the lineup and for the players to take the field," Coach Mike interjected.

"This is the day we've all been waiting for," Coach Carl stated as he held out his hand. Coach Mike, placed his hand on top of it, followed by the rest of the team. He then asked the question. "What does it mean to be a Brave?" Each of the players' faces lit up with excitement.

"Having the courage to face any opponent that comes your way without fear...Show me, my opponent!" They all yelled in unison, causing the entire crowd and visiting team to stop and take notice. They broke their huddle, then

proceeded to run out into the field to their respective positions.

Coach Mike and Coach Carl looked on proudly.

"I haven't seen that look on your face in a long-time, Coach. You look like you're back in your element and loving every minute of it," Coach Mike said.

Coach Carl took off his baseball cap, then retrieved the lineup card out of his pocket, before stating, "I am the coach of the Lincoln Park Braves. We do more than just coach kids here. We fill voids that some parents can't fill for one reason or another. Some kids' lack of a father figure in their lives, can cause self-esteem issues; the same issues that you and I both faced as kids coming up. We would be doing ourselves, our community, and these kids a great disservice if men like us didn't fulfill the duties set before us when it comes to our youth."

"I get it, Coach, and that's why I will coach here until..." He paused as something in the parking lot had gotten his attention. "Here comes Miriam, Coach."

Coach Carl turned to see Miriam jogging with her glove and her cleats in her hands. She made it to the dugout and immediately sat down to begin to get prepared for the game.

"Hey, Coach Carl and Coach Mike... As soon as I get my cleats on, I'll be ready!" she exclaimed, moving as fast as she could.

"Take your time, Miriam," Coach Carl replied.

Miriam stopped suddenly. She was now confused. "Why, Coach, the game is about to start?"

"You're right, but you won't be playing anytime soon."

Miriam slammed her cleats on the ground hard, causing them to bounce up off the cement floor.

"And that right there, Miriam, is one of the main reasons that you will be sitting to start the game. Do you even have a valid reason for being late for the game?"

"Yes, I was waiting on my dad to come in town," she answered with pride.

"Is he here?" Coach Mike questioned as he looked around.

"No," she stated barely above a whisper.

Coach Carl knew all about the disappointment Miriam had been experiencing with her dad as he had spoken with her mother. He truly believed that her dad did not intentionally try to disappoint his daughter but had little choice with being an over-the-road truck driver whose route took him all over the United States.

"Miriam, as your coach, I empathize with you. I used to look forward to my mom coming to my games, same as Coach Mike with his dad, but neither could. My mom worked to provide for my siblings and me. Attending a game would essentially be taking money out of our family's pocket. Your dad loves you a lot and he supports you playing baseball as your mom told me, but to be a part of this team, you need to be committed. We spoke at practice about dealing with adversity. This is another example of that."

"How is my dad not being here another example of overcoming adversity?"

"In the sense that if your dad didn't show up, you would still go out and perform your job to the best of your ability, right?"

"Yes."

"Although you feel disappointed, and maybe not as up to playing as you would be if he was watching, right?"

"Yes, Coach," she replied as she caught on to his message.

"Glad that you understand because today, your teammates were up against adversity," Coach Mike stated. Miriam looked out at the field in disbelief.

"Why Coach, what happened?"

"You happened, Miriam. Your teammates felt frustrated and disappointed when they didn't see you arrive in time to be placed in the line-up. You didn't fulfill your commitment to us—or your teammates—whether you think waiting on your dad to arrive is a valid reason or not," Coach Mike stated as the leadoff batter was announced for the visiting team.

They all watched intently as Justin delivered the first pitch. "Strike One!" the umpire yelled while a small cheering section began clapping. Justin caught the ball from his catcher and then glanced into the outfield before retaking the mound. He hurled another pitch straight down the plate that led to a high fly ball being launched into left-center field. The play seemed to unfold in slow motion as Desmond and Ricky ran toward each other, in an attempt to catch the flyball. Both kids quickly realized that the other was approaching and stopped suddenly. The flyball fell a few feet away from them both, then began a fast roll to the fence. The batter proceeded to run without care as he listened to his coaches guide him around the base pads, stopping him at the third base. The visiting team's dugout exploded with applause.

Miriam kicked her glove, which was lying on the floor, in a display of frustration. "Put me in the game, Coach. I would've called Ricky off and caught that ball," she stated with complete confidence.

Coach Mike and Coach Carl looked at each other as if deciding who would respond first.

"You got this one, Coach," Coach Mike told him as he walked to the end of the dugout and began to coach up his team. "Shake it off, Justin. That didn't hurt us one bit," he stated. Justin nodded his head in acknowledgment.

"Miriam, putting you in the game is not that simple. You are one of our best players, true enough, but do you think it would be right if you were out there giving it your best and I took you out of the game? Mind you, I would be removing a dedicated player from the game for someone who didn't care enough to communicate with the team that they would be late. Not only have you done this at practice, you in turn show up late for the first game of the season. Would that be fair?"

"No, it wouldn't be fair," she replied, being honest.

"It wouldn't. I do know that there was a good chance that you would have caught that ball, Miriam. But talent is not all we care about on this team; we care about being responsible and communicating. I hope that today was a teaching moment for you to know about communication and responsibility. It doesn't matter what problem may arise that causes you to change or adjust your plans after making a prior commitment. You are responsible for ensuring the party you are committed to be notified. I hope we are on the same page now, Miriam, and I'm sure I speak for your teammates as well."

Miriam processed every word that Coach Carl was telling her. She realized that she was indeed emulating her dad, with her lack of communication and disregard for others' feelings. Everything that Coach had said made perfect sense to her. She realized that if you give someone your word and cannot follow through with it, the right thing to do is call them or give them advance notice. That treating others the way that we want to be treated yields the best results. She realized that it shows others that you have good character and that you can be counted on.

"Coach, thank you for being more than a coach. If you think I don't deserve to play, I'm okay with that. From now on, I will work to earn the trust of my teammates and my coaches," Miriam stated, genuinely thankful for having coaches that cared about, more than just winning games.

The team filed into the dugout after recording the last out. They were all so excited when they saw Miriam; everyone except Ricky. Miriam noticed and walked over to him.

"Hey, good try, Ricky. It was a well-hit ball. Next time, you guys call for it the way the coaches taught us, and you will be good. You did get the ball in quick enough so that we were able to hold the runner on third base and get out of the inning without them scoring. Great job!"

Ricky's facial expression lit up. He wasn't used to being told that he did something right. "Thanks, Miriam," he stated, then took a seat on the bench. She followed him.

"I'm not going to play today, Ricky. You have earned the right to play by being at every practice and showing your commitment to this team. That is something that I haven't done yet, and today I realized why. I told Coach that I would earn my way back on the field, so they already know. Go back out there Ricky and play like you have nothing to lose." Ricky couldn't believe his ears. He looked over at Coach Carl, who had been listening to his and Miriam's conversation the entire time. Coach Carl nodded in agreeance, and then gave Miriam the thumbs up.

"I guess it's safe to say that you'll be here next season, huh, Coach?" Coach Mike questioned, already knowing the answer.

Coach Carl scanned over his players as they stood against the dugout gate to get a better view. There wasn't a place in the world that he'd rather be than coaching. He began to realize that just as much as he and Coach Mike were a big part of those kids' lives, those kids were a huge part of theirs as well.

"I'm like you, Mike—I'll be coaching until I can't anymore. My mom once told me when I was a kid in this same park... 'One day, you're going to be a good coach. A good coach that will help kids grow mentally in the right direction because you are a great leader...just like your dad.'"

FROM THE AUTHORS

I hope you enjoyed *Just Like My Dad*!

This novel was created to show the importance of male figures and their roles in children's lives. We all know that the way we are raised plays a huge part in how we live our lives. But what happens when a parent is absent or not mentally capable of raising a child with proper morals and values? This fiction adaptation shows how positive thoughts and life lessons can come from outside of the immediate family.

Coach Carl and Coach Mike could be anyone you know. There is a saying: "It takes a village to raise a child." This is a true statement. Justin had a dad in his life but his dad was not giving his son the proper tools to go through life by making him believe he was better than others. Then we take a look at Miriam, who mimicked her dad's behavior as she never committed to anything. Coach Carl, in the end, showed her just how much she was like her dad, and it gave her a new outlook on keeping her word and why it is essential. JLMD is a novel that gives you a problem scenario while providing a teachable solution that can be universal.

ELIZABETH M. JOHNSON

Brooklyn, New York-native Elizabeth Johnson is a breakout author with a promising writing career ahead of her. Signed with PlaTy Multimedia & Publishing, Elizabeth introduces her first work to the world of children's books on May 16, 2021. Her debut title, *Just Like my Dad,* is co-authored with the already well-established author, Tyrell Plair.

Elizabeth's resume boasts an Associate of Science in Early Childhood Education and an Associate of Arts in General Education and is currently pursuing her Bachelor of Science in Organizational Management.

Currently residing in Palm Bay, Florida with her husband and son, Elizabeth spends her spare time baking, watching football, traveling, honing her skills as a photographer, and volunteering in the church and her local community.

TYRELL PLAIR

Born in the windy city of Chicago, Illinois, Tyrell Plair took an interest in reading and writing at a young age, which led him to begin writing poetry for his classmates. Over the years, Tyrell honed his skills as a writer by ghostwriting novels, penning screenplays, and adding film directing to his repertoire.

In 2019 Tyrell released his debut novel "Stolen Innocence" as an independent author. He has also written and produced commercials for "Outrageous Love Foundation," "L&J Multicultural Barbershop," and other film projects.

Tyrell served his country with honor as a proud soldier in the United States Army with a tour in Kuwait. He also holds a Bachelor of Science in Applied Psychology with a Media and Technology concentration from the University of Phoenix.

When not fulfilling his role as Chief Operating Officer of Platy Multimedia, you can find Tyrell locked in on a game of chess, fishing, or enjoying his family and friends.

ALSO BY ELIZABETH

Just Like My Dad

Igual que mi Papá

Mamaw Mel's Kitchen

Follow Elizabeth:

www.facebook.com/authorlizjohnson

ALSO BY TYRELL PLAIR

Stolen Innocence

Just Like My Dad

Igual que mi Papá

Follow Tyrell:

https://www.amazon.com/Tyrell-Plair

Made in the USA
Columbia, SC
03 July 2024

38035918R00050